Today Is Your Gift, Open Your Present

R.J. MODELL

#1 BEST SELLING AUTHOR

Today Is Your Gift, Open Your Present

Written By
R.J. Modell

Book Cover & Interior Design
By David Stern & Rick Kaempfer

© Copyright 2016

First Printed, 2016

Hash Tag Publishing
ISBN-13: 978-0997101829
ISBN-10: 0997101822

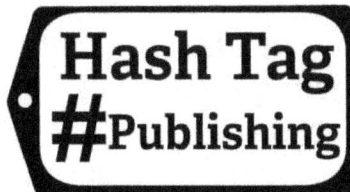

Hash Tag #Publishing

Words of Art
Hashed Between 2 Covers

Introduction

Author R.J. Modell writes words of wisdom for the heart from the heart. You may be holding this book in your hands, but it will definitely touch your heart, your soul and your life.

R.J. Modell's quotes have captivated over 5 Million readers worldwide via social media and have touched hearts around the globe. His words have been used for motivation, inspiration and encouragement in schools, colleges, hospitals, nursing homes, rehabilitation centers, mental health facilities, half way houses, funeral homes and Veteran's hospitals.

R.J. Modell is one of those rare literary talents who seems to effortlessly excel in many genres of literature. Whether it be formal business writing, children's stories, anecdotes, words of wisdom, humor, note card poetry or dramatic scripts for the stage and screen, R.J. Modell does it all, and he accomplishes it all exceptionally well.

A multitalented, creative, imaginative, highly accomplished professional writer, business leader, team builder, driving force in the community, and entrepreneur, R.J. Modell's extensive and diverse work background has played a key role in his metamorphosis as a best-selling author.

Working closely with people of all ages and providing families with compassion, guidance, love and support in their time of need, served as the springboard for his straightforward, yet deeply profound, intimate and heartfelt writing style. As an author, he has become a widely read Blogger, who has established a global fan base, via various social media sites.

R.J. Modell enthralls his readers with powerful anecdotes, creative quotes, inspiring poetry, uplifting words, lighthearted humor, messages of hope, positive images, and an underlying message to spread peace and love around the world.

With the profound soul of a seasoned poet, R.J. Modell churns out words of wisdom like a human anecdote machine, yet every word is carefully selected, crafted with precision and originates from his heart.

R.J. Modell is not just a writer, he is a literary artist. The painter creates paintings with canvas, paint and ideas. The sculptor creates sculptures with plaster, clay and talent. The literary artist creates literary art with pen, paper and imagination. R.J. Modell is the ultimate literary artist.

R.J. Modell's writing is imaginative, whimsical, innovative, thought provoking and infused with creative expression that provides an aesthetically pleasing literary banquet for readers to behold.

Enjoy this book and please take every one of this man's words to heart. R.J. Modell commands his words like a general commands his soldiers.

A Note From The Author

Your Feelings Are A Gift To Yourself
Your Feelings Belong To **YOU** Alone
Nobody Can Take Your Feelings
No One Can Change Your Feelings
Love Your Feelings
Embrace Your Feelings
Cherish Your Feelings
Accept Your Feelings
Explore Your Feelings
Value Your Feelings
Do Not Deny Your Feelings
Feel Your Feelings As Only **YOU** Can
Live Your Feelings
Your Feelings Are Forever Yours

R.J. Modell

No Restaurant Will Serve You Success On A Platter, You Have To Write Your Own Recipe, Follow It Step By Step, Serve It To Yourself And Enjoy!

Keep Away From Negative People and Bad Thoughts! You Will Be Happier and Healthier

THIS IS NOT YOUR PRACTICE LIFE, THIS IS YOUR REAL LIFE, LIVE EVERY DAY TO THE FULLEST, AND DO SOMETHING TO MAKE YOURSELF HAPPY EVERY DAY.

YOU ARE THE
MOST IMPORTANT
THING IN THE
WORLD TAKING
CARE OF YOU IS
NOT SELFISH YOU
CANNOT TAKE
CARE OF OTHERS
UNLESS YOU TAKE
CARE OF YOU
FIRST.

KEEP YOUR
DIRTY LAUNDRY
IN THE WASHER
AND
DRYER...NEVER
HANG IT OUT
TO DRY ON
SOCIAL MEDIA.

LIFE IS A HOCKEY GAME, SCORE GREAT GOALS.

If For Some
Reason You Ever
Find Yourself At
The Bottom...
Remember There Is
Only One
Direction To
Go...And That Is
Straight Up To
The Top.

IF YOU EVER
STRIKE OUT, JUST
PICK UP THE BAT,
DUST YOURSELF
OFF, AND KEEP
TRYING UNTIL
YOU HIT EVERY
HOME RUN.

Time Is Nothing More Than A Numerical Measurement of Dreams Gone By, Make The Most of Every Hour, Minute and Second.

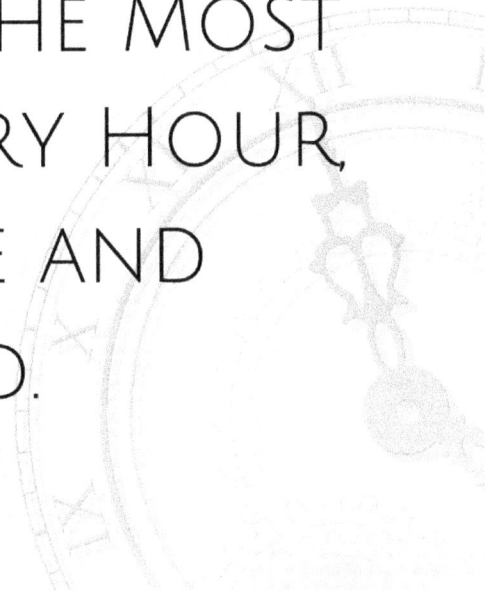

A Plane Takes Off
Very Slowly,
Then Reaches
Lofty Heights,
Think of
Yourself As A Jet,
Find Your Wings
And Soar.

Do Not Just Settle For The Stars, Reach For The Moon, Touch The Planets, And Discover New Galaxies Along The Way.

"FAMILY" IS NOT ALWAYS RELATIVES AND "RELATIVES" ARE NOT ALWAYS FAMILY.

THE LADDER
TO SUCCESS IS
ALL YOURS,
BUT BE
PREPARED TO
CLIMB HIGH.

SOME FOLKS
ARE LIKE FRESH
BAKED BREAD,
CRUSTY ON
THE OUTSIDE,
BUT WARM
AND LOVING
ON THE INSIDE.

EDUCATION IS YOUR NEEDLE AND THREAD, IT'S UP TO YOU TO WEAVE THE TAPESTRY.

Leave Yesterday's
Road Traveled
Behind, Do Not
Look Back!
Travel a New
Road Paved
With Adventure,
Embrace It and
Never Turn
Back!

No Matter How
Great You
Become, And
You Will Go
Far, Never
Forget To
Thank Those
Who Helped
You Shine Like A
Star

YESTERDAY IS
HISTORY, ALL
THAT MATTERS
IS WHO YOU
ARE TODAY,
AND WHO YOU
WILL BECOME
TOMORROW.

LIFE IS TOO SHORT TO WASTE YOUR HOURS, LIVING AMONG WEEDS INSTEAD OF FLOWERS

WHEN SOMEONE
BELIEVES IN YOU,
YOUR TALENTS AND
YOUR DREAMS AND
HELPS YOU MAKE
THEM A REALITY YOU
KNOW YOU HAVE
FOUND YOUR BEST
FRIEND FOREVER

MONEY IS IMPORTANT. MONEY BUYS THINGS WE NEED TO LIVE, BUT NEVER WORK SO HARD MAKING MONEY THAT YOU DON'T HAVE TIME TO ENJOY THE PEOPLE YOU HAVE BEEN BLESSED WITH.

WORDS ARE A
PRECIOUS GIFT,
WRITE THEM
AND SPEAK
THEM WISELY,
HANDLE THEM
WITH CARE.

CLIMB THE
HIGHEST
MOUNTAIN, GET
BACK UP IF YOU
FALL, PAINT
YOUR OWN
DESTINY, ALWAYS
STAND PROUD
AND TALL.

The Game of Life
Is Just Like Sports,
Play Hard and Let
The Chips Fall
Where They
May...If You Tried
Your Best You
Have Nothing to
Regret.

If You Are Unhappy
With The Four Walls
That Surround Your
Life, Never Ever
Forget Every Room
Has A Door, Do Not
Be Afraid To Use It, Set
Yourself Free, Work
Hard, And Become
Every Thing you Ever
Wanted To Be.

THE GREATEST GIFT YOU HAVE TO OFFER IS THE GIFT OF YOU!

It Is Not Enough To Simply Toot Your Own Horn, You Have To Show Them You Are A Rock Star!

NEGATIVE PEOPLE AND BULLIES ONLY HAVE THE POWER YOU GIVE THEM, PULL THE PLUG ON PEOPLE WITH NEGATIVE VIBES, THE POWER OUTAGE WILL LIGHT UP YOUR LIFE.

Your Talents Are Your Most Priceless Gift...Use Them Daily and Use Them Wisely.

When The Road You Walk Upon Is Paved With Jagged Rocks, Find A Way To Pave It With Gold.

You Could Be The Butterfly That Colors Our World With Peace, Come Out Of Your Cocoon and Reveal Your True Colors, As You Find Your Wings and Soar

THE ACT OF
FORGIVENESS
IS THE
GREATEST
GIFT YOU
CAN GIVE TO
YOURSELF.

UNLESS YOU ARE COVERED IN WOOL, YOU ARE NOT A SHEEP, IF YOU DO NOT LIKE THE PATH YOU ARE BEING LED DOWN, DO NOT FOLLOW!

When Someone Steals Your Thunder, Strike Back As A Bolt of Lightning... Brighter, Better and Bolder Than Ever Before!

Think of Yourself as a Magnet, Attract Positive People and Situations and Repel the Negative.

You Possess Unique Talents, Thoughts, Ideas and Gifts That Were Not Given To The Rest of Us, Discover What Makes You Uniquely You, and Make the Most of Who You Are.

There Is No Such Thing As A Hopeless Situation, Sometimes You Just Need To Reach Out To The Right People To Lend You A Hand.

Even When Times
Are Stormy, With
Courage, Faith,
Hard Work &
Discipline, You
Can Weather
Any Storm and
Rise Up To Shine
Brighter Than
The Sun.

The Best Gifts In
Life Do Not
Come With A
Price Tag, People
Who Love You
Unconditionally
Are A Priceless
Gift To Cherish
And Behold.

TEARDROPS ARE
NATURE'S WAY
OF SOOTHING
THE HEART AND
CLEANSING THE
SOUL...NEVER
BE AFRAID TO
CRY.

True Friends
Have A Lot In
Common With
Trees, They
Stand By You,
Shelter You,
Stand With
You Forever
And Never
Leave Your Side.

FIRST AND FOREMOST...BE YOUR OWN BEST FRIEND... LOVING YOURSELF IS NOT SELFISH...IT IS A NECESSITY.

If You Carry
Too Much
Baggage, Your
Life Will Be
Grounded,
Lighten The
Load of the
Past, So You
Can Soar Like A
Jet Plane.

LIFE IS LIKE A BASKETBALL GAME, WE CAN'T MAKE EVERY BASKET WE SHOOT, BUT WE WILL ALWAYS BE ABLE TO BOUNCE BACK AND SHOOT AGAIN.

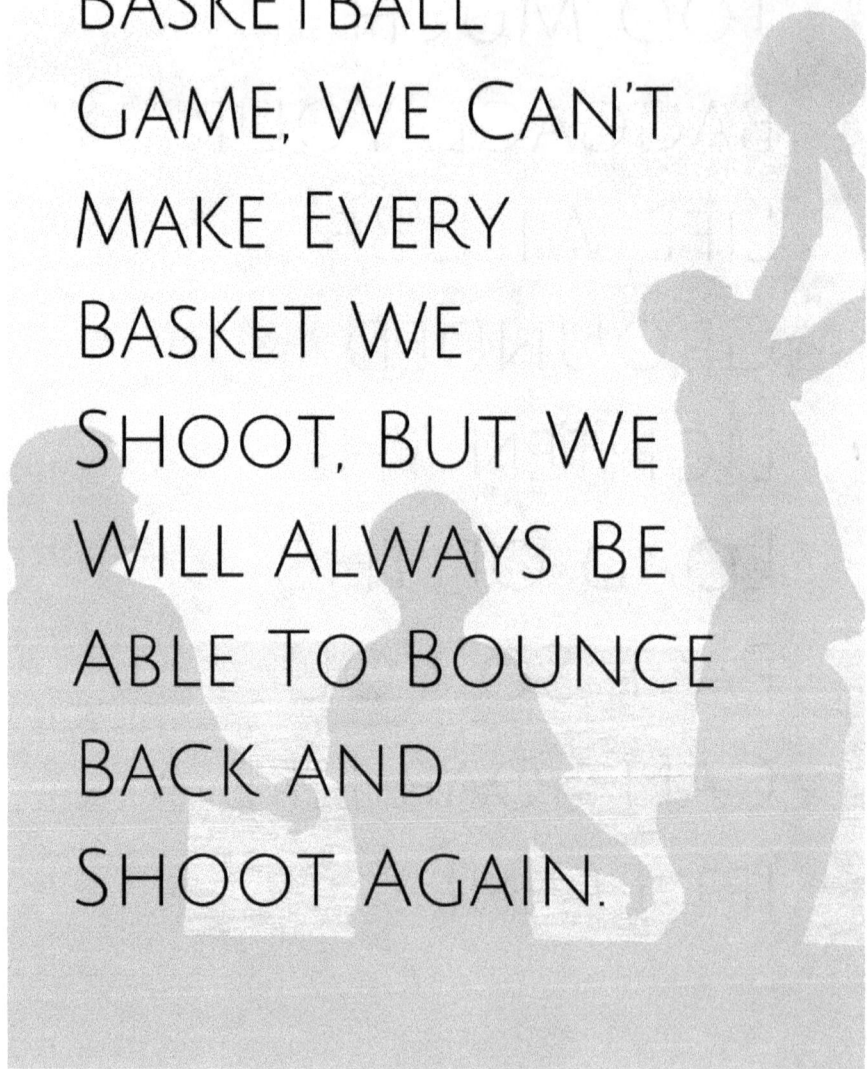

BEING
SUCCESSFUL IS
NOT A CRIME,
THE ONLY
CRIME IS NOT
TRYING TO
SUCCEED AT
ALL.

DON'T JUST
DREAM IT, DARE
TO DO IT, AND
DON'T STOP
UNTIL YOU
MAKE EVERY
WILDEST DREAM
IN YOUR HEART
A REALITY.

ALWAYS STAY
CLOSE TO
THOSE WHO
LOVE YOU, AS
REAL FRIENDS
ARE PRECIOUS
AND FEW.

You Are Too Strong of A Person To Allow Others To Shape Your Destiny, Take Control of Your Own Life, Live and Love As You Choose, And Do Whatever It Takes To Make Yourself Happy.

GREATNESS WAS
NEVER ACHIEVED
IN ONE LEAP,
TAKE SMALL
STRIDES, EVERY
STEP WILL LEAD
YOU TO
HAPPINESS,
SUCCESS AND
FULFILLMENT.

WE CAN'T
ALWAYS WIN, SO
WHEN WE LOSE,
WE MUST
HUMBLY LEARN
FROM OUR
MISTAKES, SO WE
CAN WIN NEXT
TIME AND BE A
GRACIOUS
WINNER.

Do Not Take Your Talents and Gifts To The Grave With You, Use Them Now, As None of Us Are Promised Tomorrow.

You Are
Not A
Victim of
Your
Past...You
Are A
Survivor!

All Roads Lead To Somewhere... Travel The Highway That Leads You To Happiness.

Sometimes You Simply Need To Take A Giant Leap of Faith and Know Things Will Work Out As They Were Meant To Be.

FORGET THE SILVER, GOLD AND DIAMONDS...THERE IS NO GREATER TREASURE ON THIS EARTH MORE VALUABLE AND PRICELESS THAN YOU.

In Life There Are Fake Friends and Real Friends...With Experience You Will Learn To Know The Difference.

REAL FRIENDS
ARE SO
PRECIOUS AND
FEW, BE
GRATEFUL FOR
THOSE WHO
ARE LOYAL
AND TRUE.

WE ARE ALL
EQUAL WHEN WE
ARE BORN AND
WHEN WE DIE...
WHY NOT
CELEBRATE OUR
EQUALITY ALL THE
DAYS IN
BETWEEN?

Verbal Abuse Hurts Just As Much, If Not More, Than Physical Abuse...Anyone Who Uses Their Words To Inflict Pain On You, Is Not Your REAL Friend Or Family.

YOU ARE A
GLORIOUS
LIGHT FOR ALL
TO CHERISH
AND
BEHOLD...SHINE
BRIGHT AND
NEVER ALLOW
YOUR CANDLE
TO STOP
GLOWING.

MAKE YOUR
DREAMS A
REALITY, PURSUE
EVERY ENDEAVOR,
LIVE EACH DAY
AS IF YOU WILL
LIVE FOREVER.

TODAY IS A
BRAND NEW DAY,
DO NOT LOOK
BACK AND DO
NOT FEAR, SEIZE
EACH DAY, MAKE
THE MOST OF
EVERY YEAR.

YOU ARE NOT A
PRISONER OF
YOUR PAST
CIRCUMSTANCES,
BREAK OUT OF
THAT JAIL AND
FREE YOURSELF
IN MIND, BODY,
HEART, SOUL
AND SPIRIT.

ALWAYS STAY
CLOSE TO THOSE
PEOPLE WHO MAKE
YOU FEEL LESS
ALONE, GENUINELY
HAPPY, TRULY
RESPECTED AND
UNCONDITIONALLY
LOVED.

YOU WERE
CREATED TO BE
A RAINBOW OF
HOPE...COLOR
OUR WORLD
WITH PEACE
AND LOVE.

In The Garden of
Life, People Are
Like Plants, You
Can Feed Them
and Give Them
Water, But
Without Love,
They Will Wither
and Die.

SURROUND
YOURSELF WITH
PEOPLE WHO
ENCOURAGE YOUR
DREAMS, LOVE YOU
UNCONDITIONALLY
AND ACCEPT YOU
FOR EXACTLY WHO
YOU ARE.

BEST FRIENDS
ARE THE
"FAMILY" WE
PICK FOR
OURSELVES
FROM THE
GARDEN OF
LOVE.

THE TIME IS
RIGHT FOR YOUR
INNER STAR TO
GLOW AND
SHINE BRIGHT, BE
THE GUIDING
LIGHT THAT
CHANGES THE
WORLD.

When Something
Seems Impossible,
Remember That
Anything is
Possible, With
Determination,
Ambition,
Dedication, Hard
Work and
Courage.

IF SOMEONE TELLS YOU THAT YOU "CAN'T DO" SOMETHING... SAY, "YES I CAN," GO OUT AND DO IT, AND PROVE THEIR LACK OF FAITH IN YOU WRONG!

Every Monday
Morning Is An
Opportunity
To Plant The
Seeds That
Blossom Into
A Beautiful
Week.

YOU ARE A
MAJESTIC RIVER,
KEEP RUNNING
STRONG AND
FREE, CARVING
YOUR OWN
UNIQUE PATH.

KNOWLEDGE IS A
GIFT, WHAT YOU
DO WITH YOUR
KNOWLEDGE, IS
YOUR PRESENT
TO YOURSELF,
AND THOSE
AROUND YOU.

LIFE IS TOO SHORT TO
CHASE AFTER
RELATIVES WHO DO
NOT REALLY LOVE
YOU IN RETURN,
SOMETIMES REAL
FAMILY IS STANDING
RIGHT IN FRONT OF
YOU WITH OPEN
ARMS – THOSE PEOPLE
ARE CALLED –
FRIENDS.

May Your Eyes See
Only Rainbows,
May Your Heart be
Filled With Peace,
May Your Soul Be
Warmed By
Sunlight, May
Your Happiness
Never Cease.

BE A RAY OF
HOPE, IN ALL
YOU DO AND
SAY, TO MAKE
OUR WORLD
A BETTER
PLACE, EVERY
WAKING DAY.

YOU CAN'T CHANGE YOUR PAST, BUT YOU CAN FOCUS YOUR LIFE ON LIVING HAPPY FOR TODAY, TOMORROW AND THE FUTURE.

"LOVE" IS THE ONLY LANGUAGE THE WORLD NEEDS TO SPEAK.

SOME PEOPLE WOULDN'T
KNOW A DIAMOND
FROM A ROCK, ONE
PERSON'S DIAMOND IS
ANOTHER PERSON'S
ROCK, BASK IN THE
GLOW OF THE DIAMOND
THAT IS YOU, THOSE
WHO VIEW YOUR
DIAMOND AS A ROCK
CAN GO HIDE UNDER
THEIR ROCK WHILE YOU
SPARKLE AND SHINE.

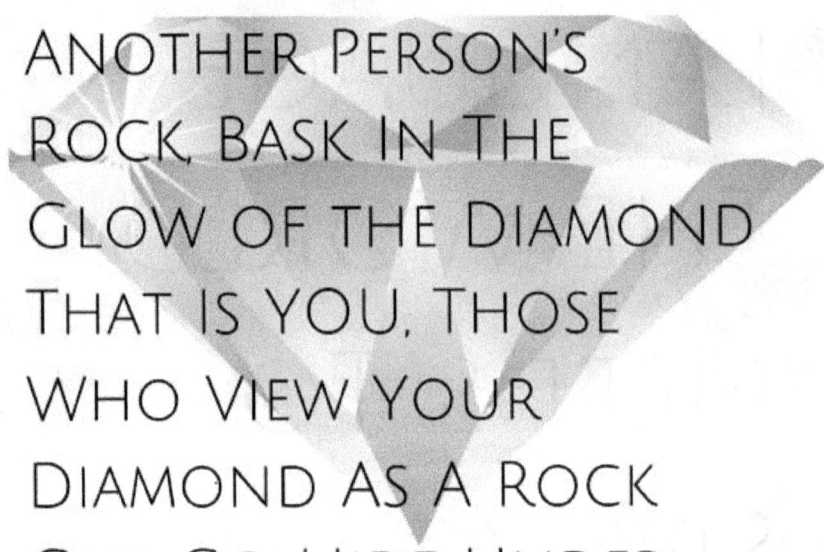

If Someone Says "I Love You" and Means It...Never Take That Person For Granted.

EVERY NEW DAY
ON THIS EARTH IS
ANOTHER NEW
BEGINNING,
ANOTHER NEW
START AND
ANOTHER
PRICELESS GIFT
JUST WAITING TO
BE UNWRAPPED.

YOU KNOW IT ISN'T
REALLY FAIR THAT SO
MUCH TALENT AND
POTENTIAL IS ALL
WRAPPED UP IN JUST
ONE PERSON...UNWRAP
YOUR GIFTS, CHANGE
YOUR LIFE FOR THE
BETTER, AND CHANGE
THE WORLD ALONG THE
WAY!

About The Author

A writer for all ages and genres, Amazon #1 Best Selling Author R.J. Modell served as the co-editor of *Queasy Street: Volume One – Eleven Tales of Fantasy*, which debuted as a #5 Best Seller for the late Joe Alaskey, an Emmy Award Winning Actor and Best Selling Author.

R.J. Modell enjoyed six weeks as the #1 Hot New Release in Children's Hockey Books for *Hock E. Puck Meets Hock E. Stick*, the first in the series *Puck and Stick: True Blue Friends Forever.*

R.J. Modell's quotations and poetry have been read around the world via various social media sites.

Fluent in business writing, fiction and non-fiction literature, sports writing, quotation writing, feature writing, children's literature, lyric writing, stage writing, screen writing and poetry.

R.J. Modell has garnered awards and praise for his writing, enjoys volunteering, and giving back to his community whenever possible. The author is a member of the Chicago Writers Association and serves as an Illinois Reads Ambassador for the Illinois Reading Council. He is a Chicago White Sox and Chicago Blackhawks Fan.

Web Links

R.J. Modell Website
http://www.RJModell.com

R.J. Modell Facebook Fan Page
http://www.Facebook.com/RJModell

Today Is Your Gift Website
http://www.TodayIsYourGiftOpenYourPresent.com

Today Is Your Gift Facebook Page
http://www.Facebook.com/TodayIsYourGiftOpenYourPresent

Puck and Stick Website
http://www.PuckandStick.com

Puck and Stick Facebook Fan Page
http://www.Facebook.com/HockEPuckMeetsHockEStick

Queasy Street Facebook Page
http://www.Facebook.com/QueasyStreet

Puck and Stick Fan Shop
http://www.CafePress.com/HockEPuckMeetsHockEStick

Chicago Author Solutions
http://www.chicagoauthorsolutions.com

Eckhartz Press
http://www.eckhartzpress.com

www.ingramcontent.com/pod-product-compliance
Lightning Source LLC
Chambersburg PA
CBHW060035050426
42448CB00012B/3019